More Than
CONQUERORS

More Than CONQUERORS

DEWEY GARDNER

Trilogy Christian Publishers

A Wholly Owned Subsidiary of Trinity Broadcasting Network

2442 Michelle Drive

Tustin, CA 92780

For information, address Trilogy Christian Publishing

Rights Department, 2442 Michelle Drive, Tustin, Ca 92780.

Trilogy Christian Publishing/ TBN and colophon are trademarks of Trinity Broadcasting Network.

For information about special discounts for bulk purchases, please contact Trilogy Christian Publishing.

Manufactured in the United States of America

Trilogy Disclaimer: The views and content expressed in this book are those of the author and may not necessarily reflect the views and doctrine of Trilogy Christian Publishing or the Trinity Broadcasting Network.

10 9 8 7 6 5 4 3 2 1

Library of Congress Cataloging-in-Publication Data is available.

ISBN 978-1-64088-571-4 (Print Book)

ISBN 978-1-64088-572-1 (ebook)

Introduction

Yet in all these things we are more than conquerors through Him who loved us.

—ROM. 8:37

The eighth chapter of Romans is the great chapter on the doctrine of the victorious life and security for believers. In verse 37, we find the bold statement that we are more than conquerors through Him who loved us. A conqueror is one who overcomes his enemy. To be "more than" a conqueror, then, must be one who goes beyond defeating his enemy. We will find in this eighth chapter of the book of Romans a marvelous revelation of truth which will substantiate Paul's bold claim that believers are indeed "more than conquerors through Him who loved us," as well as evidence that will convince us, just as it did the apostle, that nothing anywhere and at any time can separate us from "the love of God which is in Christ Jesus our Lord."

Those who are familiar with the Bible know that, after all is consummated according to the will of God, in the conclusion of all things, those who belong to Christ are the winners. However, the same Bible also teaches that we may live that victorious life at this present time. If we are to experience such a life, we must see things as they are in the spirit, not as they appear to be from an earthly point of view. We must see ourselves (as we truly are) seated in heavenly places in Christ, far above all principalities and spiritual forces in the heavenlies; that we are no longer enslaved to sin and passions of the flesh. Our life must be one of faith in God, not one striving for holiness by keeping regulations and requirements of the law; of following religious rules and rituals; but that of living the victorious life by faith in Christ.

The Christian life, according to the New Testament, is not one of struggling and self-effort, of trying and failing, of doing the best we can, expecting the Lord to forgive our shortcomings. The real Christian life described in the New Testament is Christ, Himself, living in and through the believer by the indwelling Spirit of Christ who is now joined with our human spirit. Our part, as believers, is to trust in, rely upon, and cooperate with the indwelling spirit of life.

The Christian life is a totally new life lived in the spirit as opposed to the old life which was lived according to the flesh. In His plan of redemption, God did not merely "renovate" our old life, give us a fresh start, and expect us to keep His law from here on out. The Gospel of the New Covenant is that "our old man was crucified with Christ and buried with Him," thus taking care of the man of sin and of flesh, but beyond that, there is the Good News that we were "raised in Him" as part of the "new creation," "created in righteousness and true holiness!" (That is, in our spirit.) And that isn't all; we read that "He raised us up together with Him and seated us with Him in the heavenlies."

These are all New Testament realities which, being spiritual, only affect our inner attitudes and outward actions when they become revelation knowledge and are activated by faith. The work of the Holy Spirit is to reveal these spiritual realities to our hearts and minds. We receive them by faith. He also takes us through different situations and experiences which are designed to bring us to the end of self-reliance and to dependence upon the Lord.

If we are to understand what it means to be "more than conquerors" (and how we came to be such), we must consider the statement in its context—that is, in its relation to the verses which are before it and those which follow. In this case, we should look at this statement in the light of the entire eighth chapter of the book of Romans. Much of what is stated above is taken from Romans chapter 8 and Ephesians chapters 1 through 3. Some of what will be said in the following is from the Gospel of John and of Romans chapters 3 through 7. Please be familiar with these chapters as we proceed.

Note that according to our text in Romans 8:37, it is "in all these things" that we are more than conquerors and that it is "through Him who loved us." What things? Those listed in verse 35 as things which cannot "separate us from the love of Christ"—tribulation, distress, persecution, famine, nakedness, peril, and sword. These are enemies in that they are things which are against us. We, as believers, go through such things while we are in this world. If these things cannot separate us from the love of Christ, they cannot defeat us.

The statement, "Nay, in all these things we are more than conquerors through Him that loved us" (Rom. 8:37, KJV) is in answer to the question posed in verse 35: "Who shall separate us from the love of Christ? Shall tribulation, or distress, or persecution, or famine, or nakedness, or peril, or sword?" and is an application of the quote from Psalm 44:22, "For thy sake we are killed all the day long; we are accounted as sheep for the slaughter" (KJV). It is also the conclusion the apostle has reached because of the remarkable spiritual truths he has just written.

Let us consider, once again, what being "more than conqueror" means. Being a conqueror would mean the believer wins the battle over these things (tribulation, distress, persecution, famine, nakedness, peril, and sword) and, therefore, does not come under them. He confronts the enemy, defeats him, and is declared the winner. Being more than a conqueror means the believer is not delivered from these things but goes through them, yet is not adversely affected by them but, rather, is better off from having endured them.

To illustrate the difference between one who is a "conqueror" from one who is "more than conqueror," let us use the last item in the list (the sword) as an example. It is obvious the sword here means to be put to death. The conqueror is one who engages his enemy in battle, defeats the enemy, and does not die. The "more than conqueror" is one who, although slain with the sword, comes out the greater winner.

Those who are faithful to Christ "unto death" are promised "a crown of life" (Rev. 2:10). Thousands of believers have been "slain with the sword" because they refused to renounce the name of Christ and, as a result, will receive "a better resurrection!"

Let us be thankful for those who "through faith subdued kingdoms, worked righteousness, obtained promises, stopped the mouths of lions, quenched the violence of fire, escaped the edge of the sword, out of weakness were made strong, became valiant in battle, turned to flight the armies of aliens, women (who) received their dead raised to life again" (Heb. 11:23–34). But let us not forget the "others" who "were tortured, not accepting deliverance," that they might "obtain a better resurrection," and still others who, "had trials of mockings and scourgings, yes, and of chains and imprisonment." And "those who were stoned, sawn in two, and who were slain with the sword, were sorely tried, wandered about in sheepskins and goatskins, were destitute, afflicted, tormented" (those to whom is ascribed the glorious and eternal accolade "of whom the world was not worthy!") (Heb. 11:35–37.) These all "died in faith" and are presently waiting for the resurrection and the glory that shall be revealed. They are "more than conquerors."

Romans 8:37 is not written as an encouragement to believers to help us to be more than conquerors nor is it a promise that we shall eventually become such, but is a bold statement that those who are believers in Christ are "more than conquerors through Him who loved us." However, we are more than conquerors only "through Him who loved us!" It has nothing to do with self-effort or self-sacrifice. It is through what He has done for us; what He is now doing in us; what He is accomplishing through us; and what the result shall be when He has finished His work. It is all the work of Christ for the glory of God.

Believers are "more than conquerors" because, in His infinite love, the Father watches over those who are His own. Nothing can harm them because He turns everything that comes their way to work for their good. "And we know that all things work together for good to those who love God, to those who are the called according to His purpose" (Rom. 8:28). We may not be able to see how this (whatever it is) is working for our good, but our

Father knows exactly what is needed to conform us into the likeness of His Son—His eternal purpose and goal. Being made into the likeness of His beloved Son, Jesus, is the very best thing that could happen to us. He makes everything work for our good because we love Him and are the called according to His purpose.

Let us, then, as believers, rely upon His wisdom, rest in His love, and enjoy the trip. We will find in Romans chapter 8 grounds for complete assurance which will serve as an anchor for our souls.

My purpose in the following pages is to point to the spiritual realities recorded in the eighth chapter of the book of Romans which will explain why and how believers are more than conquerors in order to convince us that absolutely nothing shall be able to separate us from the love of God which is in Christ Jesus our Lord, and, being thus persuaded, we may live confidently, victoriously, and joyfully, giving glory to His name.

Table of Contents

BELIEVERS HAVE A NEW STANDING 11

BELIEVERS HAVE A NEW DYNAMIC 23

BELIEVERS ARE A NEW CREATION 31

BELIEVERS ARE BORN OF GOD 37

WE ARE SAVED IN THIS HOPE 43

GROANINGS 53

CLOSING ARGUMENTS 61

BELIEVERS HAVE A NEW STANDING

There is therefore now no condemnation to those who are in Christ Jesus.

—Rom. 8:1

Jesus said, "He who believes in Him [the Son of God] is not condemned; but he who does not believe is condemned already, because he has not believed in the name of the only begotten Son of God. And this is the condemnation, that light has come into the world, and men loved darkness rather than light, because their deeds were evil" (John 3:18–19).

Every human being exists in one or other of the states referred to here by the Lord Jesus. One is the standing of being not condemned and the other is that of being condemned. What makes the difference is that one class are those who believe in Him; that is, they have placed their trust in Him as their Savior, and the others have not.

The status of all unbelievers is that of condemnation. They are not awaiting a trial at some point in the future to determine whether they are guilty or not; they stand before God already condemned. All have sinned and fallen short of the glory of God. Future judgment is not to determine guilt or innocence but for sentencing to just punishment.

The word "condemn" means different things depending upon its usage. The judge may condemn a thief who is guilty of robbery and sentence him to ten years in prison. The same judge may condemn a murderer to be executed. The condemnation spoken of by Jesus in John 3:18 is condemnation to death. Adam had been warned that eating of the fruit of the tree of the knowledge of good and evil would result in death the day he ate thereof. The wages of sin being death (Rom. 6:23), Adam died toward God the day he partook of that fruit.

The entire human race consisted of two people—Adam and Eve. When these two were alienated from God, the entire race was alienated. The law of procreation is that every created thing produces after its own kind; therefore, Adam and Eve could only produce children who were alienated from God with hearts which were sinful just like theirs.

Being alienated from God, mankind was exposed to another spirit being, the prince of the power of the air. Paul speaks of this in his letter to the Ephesians:

"And you He made alive, who were dead in trespasses and sins, in which you once walked according to this world, according to the prince of the power of the air, the spirit who now works in the sons of disobedience, among whom also we all once conducted ourselves in the lusts of our flesh and of the mind, and were by nature the children of wrath just as the others" (Eph. 2:1–3).

In this passage, Paul is describing the method and means by which God saves us from the situation into which we, as the fleshly descendants of Adam, were born, but he also reveals the very serious nature of the condition into which man's fall from God has left him. In his fallen state, man is exposed to the evil prince of the power of the air. He is attached to a world system which is opposed to God, and he is enslaved to the passions of his flesh.

Eating of the forbidden fruit was an act of disobedience which alienated man from his Creator, but this was only the tip of the iceberg. Man had not only sinned, he had now become a sinner by nature. He had received the spirit of lawlessness which now dwelt within him. He was no longer the submissive servant of the Lord, but a slave to sin.

Through sin, man had lost his relationship of friendship with God and also his stewardship of partnering with Him as governor of the things of Earth. He is no longer God's faithful servant.

Let us be reminded that man did not create himself nor did he just come into being. He was created by God in His image and likeness for the high and lofty purpose of reflecting and representing his Creator. He was created by and for God. Man's sense of well-being (happiness, fulfillment, contentment, peace) is not found in seeking to please himself but in pleasing his Creator. Every moment lived for self and every action performed to please or enhance self becomes a debt which is owed to the One who created us for Himself. We can never stand before the Lord with a clear conscience while this debt remains unpaid. Since we owe one hundred percent of all that we are and all that we have, there is no way we can produce a surplus which could be used to pay our debt.

To fall short of what we were created to be is to sin against the One who created us. (The definition of one of the words translated "sin" is "to miss the mark, to fall short.") Man (mankind) was created to honor and serve the Lord.

Man was given the responsible position of authority over the other creatures as God's representative and is destined to have dominion over the works of God's hands. Such great a responsibility requires absolute submission and exact obedience to the Lord. Man was to rule according to God's will, not his own. He was to depend upon the Lord for information and instruction. When man exercised his own will, against the will of God, he was out of order. He had gone astray. He had turned to his own way. (See Isa. 53:6)

The consequences of man's act of disobedience are immeasurable. The immediate result of his disobedience was spiritual death. Meaning, man's spirit (the part of man which relates to God who is Spirit) was no longer able to function in relation to God because of guilt. The continuing result is that man is now without strength or ability to recover himself.

Man has become defiled and is no longer able to serve the Lord as His representative on Earth. Being alienated from God (the source of life and goodness), man is "dead in trespasses and in sin" (Eph. 2:1) and is walking "according to the course of this world, according to the prince of the power of the air, the spirit who now works in the sons of disobedience," and is "fulfilling the desires of the flesh and of the mind" (Eph. 2:2–3). Man cannot serve God acceptably because he is corrupt, and every thought and action originates from himself and is designed, in one way or another, to enhance, protect, exalt, or please himself.

In his natural state (the condition into which he is born), man is hopeless and helpless. He is without God, enslaved to sin, part of a world which is opposed to God, and exposed to a cruel, lawless tyrant.

Man has also transgressed the law of God which requires that every transgression and act of disobedience receive a just recompense of reward. (See Heb. 2:2) Justice will be done! Right must prevail! The eternal scales of justice must be balanced! For justice to prevail, sin must be punished. The Judge of all the Earth must do right.

The condemnation, however, according to the words of Jesus, is compounded by the fact that light has come into the world, and men love darkness rather than light.

"And this is the condemnation, that light has come into the world, and men loved darkness rather than light, because their deeds were evil" (John 3:19).

By considering this verse in its context in the third chapter of the Gospel of John, we can discover the seriousness of this condemnation.

> And as Moses lifted up the serpent in the wilderness, even so must the Son of Man be lifted up, that whoever believes in Him should not perish but have eternal life.
>
> For God so loved the world that He gave His only begotten Son, that whoever believes in Him should not perish but have everlasting life. For God did not send His Son into the world to condemn the world, but that the world through Him might be saved.
>
> He who believes in Him is not condemned; but he who does not believe is condemned already, because he has not believed in the only begotten Son of God. And this is the condemnation, that the light has come into the world, and

*men loved darkness rather than light, because their deeds
were evil. For everyone practicing evil hates the light and
does not come to the light, lest his deeds should be exposed.
But he who does the truth comes to the light, that his deeds
may be clearly seen, that they have been done in God.*

—*JOHN 3:14–21*

God did not send His Son to judge (condemn) the world
but that the world, through Him, might be saved. Jesus
came as a way out for man. There was no way man
could get out of his hopeless condition of sin, death, and
judgment. Jesus is God's way of redemption of fallen man
and his lost estate. Jesus is God's way of justifying sinners
without violating His own law. Because of what Jesus did,
God can justify the ungodly and Himself be just. (Rom.
3:26).

Jesus is the Good Shepherd laying His life down for the
sheep; He is the Great Shepherd of the sheep becoming
God's Sacrifice Lamb!

God loved the sin-cursed world so much that He gave
His only begotten Son to become the Son of Man that
He might become an offering for sin. Jesus, the perfect
man—the One in whom the Father was well pleased—
the Holy One of God was made an offering for sin. This
was the arrangement made by the triune God (Father,
Son, and Holy Spirit) in a determinate counsel before He
began the beginning. This is what Peter referred to in his
message to those who had been instrumental in crucifying
the Lord Jesus:

"Ye men of Israel, hear these words; Jesus of Nazareth,
a man approved of God among you by miracles and

wonders and signs, which God did by him in the midst of you, as you yourselves also know: Him, being delivered by the determinate counsel and foreknowledge of God, ye have taken, and by wicked hands have crucified and slain" (Acts 2:22–23, KJV).

The crucifixion of Jesus Christ was the fulfillment of what the shedding of the blood of animal sacrifices had only foreshadowed as types. The millions of animals which had been slain as sacrifices for sin, from in the Garden of Eden until the crucifixion of Jesus, and the shedding of their blood could not take away sin. They were only shadows of the Lamb of God who would take away our sins.

"For it is not possible that the blood of bulls and goats could take away sins. Therefore, when He came into the world, He said: 'Sacrifice and offering You did not desire, but a body You have prepared for Me. In burnt offerings and sacrifices for sin You had no pleasure. Then I said, "Behold – In the volume of the book it is written of Me—to do Your will O God."'" (Heb. 10:4–7).

The cross is the Lord making His soul an offering for sin, for "all we like sheep have gone astray; we have turned, everyone, to his own way; and the Lord has laid on Him the iniquity of us all." "Yet it pleased the Lord [it was the Lord's choice] to bruise Him [in our stead]." (Isa. 53:6, 10).

"For He [God] made Him [Christ] who knew no sin to be sin for us [sinners] that we might become the righteousness of God in Him" (2 Cor. 5:21).

"God was in Christ reconciling the world to Himself, not imputing their trespasses to them" (2 Cor. 5:17).

Finite human beings will probably never know the full gravity of what happened that night in the Garden of Gethsemane—that night before Jesus's crucifixion and the horror He faced. It all centers around the cup which His Father gave Him. The strong words used to describe Jesus's reaction to the contents of that cup might give us a glimpse of how awful it was, and what it cost Him to obey the Father.

The words and phrases used to describe Jesus's reaction to the contents of the cup as recorded in Mathew, Mark, and Luke are very revealing. Matthew tells us that as Jesus approached His place of prayer, "He began to show grief and distress of mind and was deeply depressed" (Matt. 26:37, AMP). He said to those who were with Him, "My soul is very sad and deeply grieved, so that I am almost dying of sorrow" (Matt. 26:38, AMP).

The words recorded in the Gospel of Mark are even more graphic: "And He took with Him Peter and James and John, and began to be struck with terror and amazement and deeply troubled and depressed. And He said to them, 'My soul is exceedingly sad [overwhelmed with grief] so that it almost kills Me.'" (Mark 14:33–34, AMP).

His prayer to His Father is also revealing. He had never prayed like this before. "He fell on the ground and kept praying that if it were possible the [fatal] hour might pass from Him. And He was saying, 'Abba, [which means] Father, everything is possible for You. Take away this cup from Me; yet not what I will, but what You [will]'" (Mark. 35,36, AMP).

We are told that He prayed three times. An angel from heaven came to strengthen Him so He would not die short of Calvary. So great was His agony that He sweat great drops of blood which fell to the ground!

(Let us rest assured that if there was any other way possible, the Father would have used it!)

What was in that cup that caused our Savior such pain and agony? It had to be more than dying the painful death on the cross. Others were dying that death. Crucifixion was the normal way the Romans put to death those they considered a threat to their domination. Jesus had probably seen men being killed in that manner. He had referred to it as the way He knew His death would come. That was no shock to Him.

But when He became aware of the contents of the cup His Father had given to Him, He was shocked at the horror it contained. He was horrified! Nothing had ever troubled Him like this. This was almost more than He could handle.

That cup contained the sum of all the sins of all men for all time. In that cup was all the cruelty, the perversion, the hatred, the lying, the cheating, etc. that has ever been (or ever shall be) contrived and practiced by the people who have (or shall) inhabit planet Earth. It is impossible to imagine all the evil done in body, soul, and spirit of man, but it was all in that cup with all the punishment it deserved. It was all there in that cup which Jesus was being asked to drink.

Remember, this is the One who was always obedient to His Father, the One who knew no sin, the One in whom the Father is well pleased, the One who is altogether lovely, the Holy One of God; and He is being asked to take unto Himself all the filth, all the cruelty, and the total depravity of the human race, as well as all the punishment it deserved. He knew that, if He took that cup, He would be temporarily separated from His Father; He would be "smitten of God and afflicted." He would be "wounded for our transgressions and bruised for our iniquities."

> *Himself bore our sins in His own body on the tree" (1 Pet. 2:24). "All we like sheep have gone astray; we have turned everyone to his own way; and the Lord hath laid on Him the iniquity of us all.*
>
> —*Isa. 53:6*

> *Therefore, if anyone is in Christ, he is a new creation; old things have passed away; behold, all things have become new. Now all things are of God, who has reconciled us to Himself through Christ, and has given us the ministry of reconciliation, that is, that God was in Christ reconciling the world to Himself, not imputing their trespasses to them, and has committed to us the word of reconciliation.*
>
> —*2 Cor. 5:17–19*

Reconciliation has been made. All who will may come to God by faith in His Son. All that is required is that we come into the light allowing our deeds to be made manifest, confess our need of the Savior, trusting Him for our salvation. When we receive Jesus as our Lord and Savior, He is made unto us righteousness; we are made the righteousness of God in Him, and He, by His Spirit, comes to reside in our heart, and we are created new in Christ.

"Therefore, as by one man's offence judgment came to all men, resulting in condemnation, even so through one

Man's righteous act the free gift came to all men resulting in justification of life, for as by one man's disobedience many were made [constituted] sinners, so also by one Man's obedience many will be made [constituted] righteous" (Rom. 5:18–19).

There is, therefore, now no condemnation to those who are in Christ. We stand before God justified. (Just as if we had never sinned.)

Unbelievers are outside of Christ and are, therefore, still condemned. No one is required to remain in that condition. Everyone on Earth is invited to come into the light. God has revealed Himself to everyone. If they love their own sinful way more than they love God's light, they will not come out of their darkness into His light. The Lord has prepared the banquet at His own expense and has invited everyone to come. Those who refuse His gracious invitation are justly condemned for two reasons—one, they are yet in their sins; and two, (which is even worse) light has come into the world, and they love their darkness more than His light.

How serious it is to either neglect or reject God's gift of salvation which He has provided for us by His grace. We were redeemed from our "aimless conduct received from [our] fathers with the precious blood of Christ, as of a lamb without blemish and without spot" (1 Pet. 1:18–19). For us to reject (or to neglect or refuse to accept) deliverance through such a provision is to sin against the greatest possible love.

Those who disregarded God's provision under the law of Moses but presumptuously continued in their self-willed way "died without mercy on the testimony of two or three witnesses. Of how much worse punishment, do you suppose, will he be thought worthy who has trampled the Son of God under foot, counted the blood of the covenant by which he was sanctified a common thing, and insulted the Spirit of grace" (Heb. 10:29).

For those who have humbly accepted God's provision and way of redemption; for those who have been created new in Christ Jesus, there is no condemnation. We are more than conquerors through Him who loves us.

2

BELIEVERS HAVE A
NEW DYNAMIC

*For the law of the Spirit of life in Christ Jesus has made
me free from the law of sin and death. For what the law
could not do in that it was weak through the flesh, God
did by sending His own Son in the likeness of sinful flesh,
on account of sin: He condemned sin in the flesh, that the
righteous requirement of the law might be fulfilled in us
who do not walk according to the flesh but according to
the Spirit.*

—Rom. 8:2–4

The second New Testament reality in Romans 8 which
assures that believers are more than conquerors is that
God has given to us His Holy Spirit as our new life source.
He did not leave us to live in our own strength, but He
gave us a new power source (dynamic). This new dynamic
is the "Spirit of life in Christ Jesus" which is given to us the
moment we become believers. This is God's answer to the
question raised in Romans chapter seven, "O wretched
man that I am! Who will deliver me from this body of
death" (Rom. 7:24)?

This problem in man is described as "another law"
working in opposition to the law of God, "waring against
my mind, and bringing me into captivity to the law of
sin which is in my members" (Rom. 7:23). The law of
sin works in this manner: when God commands us what
we are to do or what we are not to do, sin (the rebellious

spirit residing within us)—rising up in opposition to God's law—causes us to do opposite of what is commanded. This law of sin brings us into captivity so that "the good that I will to do, I do not do; but the evil I will not to do, that I practice" (Rom. 7:19). This is truly a wretched condition; knowing how the Lord wants us to live, wanting to do what is right, but not being able to perform.

Through this frustrating experience, man should be aware of two things. One, sin is always present in the flesh. And two, no good thing is in the flesh. Therefore, man cannot please God by the works of the flesh; he cannot save himself. Salvation must come from another source.

Man is not able to live by the righteous standards of the law of Moses because of the weakness of the flesh. Man was never intended to live on his own without God. He was intended to be a vessel (container) in which the Spirit of God could live, making man an expression of God. He was created in God's likeness and image (godlike) so that the Spirit of God would "fit" into him.

Man is weak because he is of the flesh—fleshly. This condition came about through the fall of man when he disobeyed God. In this fall, man's heart (from whence comes the motives and intentions) was corrupted. He became ungodly (ungodlike). His conscience (part of his heart) was defiled with guilt, making him feel unwelcome in God's presence and unfit as a container of God. Man's spirit (the part of man which was designed to contain the Spirit of God) became dormant. Man was separated from God (dead in trespasses and in sin). All the strength he now had to keep God's commands was the strength of his soul (his mind, will, and emotions). He was not able to perform the righteous demands of the law because his heart (made up of the mind and emotions of the soul plus the conscience of his spirit) was corrupt (perverted) from doing things God's way to please Him, to doing things his own way, to please himself. Even when he does what the Lord says to do, he does it because he himself is pleased to do so. Man was no longer "godly" but "fleshly," that is, of the flesh.

Anything that originates with the flesh is unacceptable to God. Religious ceremonies and self-righteous good deeds are an abomination to Him. God is holy and can only accept that which is holy. Jesus is the Holy One of God. He is God's Anointed (Christ, Messiah, Deliverer, Savior). Salvation is totally of the Lord. He did the works for us for our redemption; He works within us for our sanctification; He works on our behalf for our security; and He will manifest Himself through us for our glory. Any work we do to help save ourselves only detracts from Him and infers that His works are insufficient. Our part is to believe in Him (have faith in Him, which faith is also a gift from Him). Good works which are involved in our salvation are all of Him. The good works which believers do are not in order to acquire salvation but, rather, the results of it.

"For by grace you have been saved through faith, and that not of yourselves; it is the gift of God, not of works, lest anyone should boast. For we are His workmanship, created in Christ Jesus for good works, which God prepared beforehand that we should walk in them" (Eph. 2:8–10).

Notice that according to this verse, we are not created for good works, in general, but specifically for the good works which God prepared for us to walk in—that is, the works of Christ through which He glorified His Father. In fact, it is Christ who, by His Spirit, now lives in and through believers to do those works. Paul said, "I live; yet not I but Christ liveth in me" (Gal. 2:20, KJV).

This is all part of God's great plan of redemption. The word "redeem" means "to buy back." Three Greek words in the New Testament are translated "redemption" or "to redeem." One of these words simply means "to purchase in the market place by paying the price." The second means "to purchase and remove the purchased item from the market never to be sold again." (We will refer to this usage in the next chapter).

A third word translated "redeem" means "to loose (to set free)." The redeemer must pay every incumbrance against the enslaved and must also use whatever force necessary to set him free. The enslaved does not free himself; the redeemer does. This Greek word (meaning to loose) is translated "redeem" in the following verses of scripture:

> *Looking for the blessed hope and glorious appearing of our great God and Savior Jesus Christ, who gave Himself for us, that He might redeem us from every lawless deed and purify for Himself His own special people, zealous for good works.*
>
> —*Tit. 2:13–14*

> *Knowing that you were not redeemed with corruptible things, like silver or gold, from your aimless conduct received by tradition from your fathers, but with the precious blood of Christ, as of a lamb without blemish and without spot.*
>
> —*1 Pet. 1:18–19*

God's plan of redemption was designed to restore man to godliness (godlikeness) and to the eternal purpose for which he was created (that of being a spiritual container in which God could dwell). God's redemptive plan does not merely restore man to what he was in Adam (the first man) but makes him a new creation in Christ Jesus (the second Man). By placing the Spirit of Christ within the spirit of man, He regenerates (makes alive) man's human spirit, giving him strength far beyond what Adam ever possessed. Adam was of the Earth (earthly) and could only transmit earthly life. Jesus—the second man, the Lord from heaven—is made a life-giving Spirit who gives eternal life (the same quality of life God, Himself, lives) to those who are in Him. This indwelling spirit of life is the believer's new dynamic (energy source).

God has no problem living righteously (doing the things required by the law) because that is the quality of His life; that is the kind of life that is in Him. Man does not possess this type of life by nature, it is the gift of God. Jesus Christ (the man) did not live on His own. He chose to live by the life of the Father who was in Him. He said, "Most assuredly, I say to you, the Son can do nothing of Himself, but what He sees the Father do; for whatever He does, the Son also does in like manner" (John 5:19). He also explained to His followers how He lived and the power by which He did the works which He did.

"Do you not believe that I am in the Father, and the Father in Me? The words that I speak to you I do not speak on my own authority; but the Father who dwells in Me does the works" (John 14:10).

The dynamic (energy source) by which Jesus lived was the Spirit of the Father (the Holy Spirit) who dwelt within Him. He laid His own self-life (soul) down in order to live by the Spirit of His Father. Jesus did not think for Himself; He did not live for His own pleasure; and He did not make choices for Himself. His prayer in the Garden of Gethsemane, "Not my will, but Thine be done," was characteristic of His entire life. He was always bearing His cross. He also said we must do the same if we would be His disciples. We must "lay our life [soul-life] down," "take up our cross," and "follow Him."

> *For if you live according to the flesh you will die; but if by the Spirit you put to death the deeds of the body, you will live.*
>
> —ROM. *8:13*

> *I say then: "Walk in the Spirit, and you will not fulfill the lusts of the flesh. For the flesh lusts against the Spirit, and the Spirit against the flesh; and these are contrary to one another, so that you do not do the things that you wish. But if you are led by the Spirit, you are not under the law."*
>
> —GAL. *5:16–18*

When we attempt to keep the law (by self-effort), we set aside (frustrate KJV) the grace of God by which He makes us righteous. The true Christian life is described by Paul in his epistle to the Galatians:

> *For if I build again those things which I destroyed, I make myself a transgressor. For I through the law died to the law that I might live unto God. I have been crucified with Christ; it is no longer I who live, but Christ lives in me; and the life I now live in the flesh I live by faith in the Son*

*of God, who loved me and gave Himself for me. I do not
set aside the grace of God; for if righteousness comes by the
law, then Christ died in vain.*

—GAL. 2:18–21

In this epistle, Paul is correcting the error which was being
taught to these believers. The error was that believers
must be circumcised and keep the law. Paul asked them
this question: "This only I want to learn from you: did you
receive the Spirit by the works of the law, or by the hearing
of faith? Are you so foolish? Having begun in the Spirit,
are you now being made perfect by the flesh" (Gal. 3:2–3)?

The answer to the question is obvious: God began man's
salvation by His Spirit, and He will complete it by His
Spirit. Every aspect of salvation is by grace through faith.
The reason the Spirit of Christ came to abide within the
believer is to make the things of Christ experiential in the
believer's life. He does this by living the Christ life through
the believer. For this to happen, the believer must stop
living the self-life and live by faith in Christ. This is done
by considering himself dead to sin, crucified with Christ,
but alive unto God by our having been raised in Him.

The righteous requirement of the law is fulfilled in us as
we walk in His Spirit of life. We walk by taking one step
of obedience after the other as He directs. Just as Jesus
did only what He saw the Father do, and as His Father
did the works in Him, so now, we live by the power of His
Spirit-life.

This is the provision of the New Covenant in His blood:
"I will put My law in their minds, and write it on their
hearts, and I will be their God, and they shall be My

people. No more shall every man teach his neighbor, and every man his brother, saying, 'Know the Lord,' for they shall all know me, from the least of them to the greatest of them, says the Lord. For I will forgive their iniquity, and their sin I will remember no more" (Jer. 31:33–34).

This New Covenant reality of the indwelling Spirit of life in Christ Jesus is the guarantee that those who place their trust in the Lord are more than conquerors!

BELIEVERS ARE A NEW CREATION

But you are not in the flesh but in the Spirit, if indeed the Spirit of God dwells in you.

—Rom. 8:9

Believers are not part of the old creation (the chaotic, sin-cursed world of the old man in fallen Adam) but are God's new man, created new in Christ Jesus. We are the church ("ekklesia," the called out) of the living God. We are called out of the world, unto Christ, to constitute His body of which He is Head.

Jesus said to those whom He had called to follow Him, "If you were of the world, the world would love its own. Yet because you are not of the world, but I chose you out of the world, therefore the world hates you" (John 15:19). They were left in the world as His witnesses, but they were not of the world. The actual separation came through the cross by which they were crucified unto the world, and the world was crucified unto them (Gal. 6:14). Through death and resurrection, believers are placed in an entirely different realm. Spiritually, they are seated with Christ in the heavenlies.

"But God, who is rich in mercy, because He loved us, even when we were dead in trespasses, made us alive together with Christ [by grace you are saved], and raised us up together, and made us sit together in the heavenly places in Christ Jesus" (Eph. 2:4–6).

This verse does not say we shall be raised and made to sit in the heavenly places but that we were raised together with Him and that we are now seated in heavenly places in Christ Jesus. This is a spiritual reality which can only be seen by faith as it is revealed to us by the Holy Spirit.

In the same way, the spiritual truth that we are not in the flesh but in the Spirit, can only be seen by faith as it is revealed by the Holy Spirit. Faith is "the substance [substantiation] of things hoped for, the evidence [proof] of things not seen" (Heb. 11:1).

Faith is what makes things which are real in the spirit realm effectual in the natural realm. When God speaks, He says what is true. (God cannot lie.) Faith is response to what He has said because we have confidence in Him and believe that what He has promised, He is able to do. Therefore, when God says our old man was crucified with Christ and that we are freed from enslavement to sin, faith believes God, releasing Him to make it real in the natural.

Just as believers are set apart from this present evil world (a system which is opposed to God's rule) and are not part of it but are left in it to be His witnesses to it, so are we left in these natural bodies but freed from the lusts of the flesh.

Jesus said to Nicodemus, "Most assuredly, I say to you, unless one is born again, he cannot see the kingdom of God" (John 3:3).

Nicodemus, thinking only in the natural, questioned, "How can a man be born when he is old? Can he enter a second time into his mother's womb and be born?"

Jesus responded, saying to Nicodemus, "Most assuredly, I say to you, unless one is born of water and the Spirit, he cannot enter the kingdom of God."

The kingdom of God is spiritual and can only be entered by a spiritual birth. Heavenly things (spiritual realities) are not received by the natural mind; they are spiritually understood as they are revealed by the Holy Spirit. They are received by our renewed spirit. They affect our outward conduct as they are revealed to our spirit and our mind is renewed by them.

The outward conduct of the believer is changed, not by observance of the letter of the law but by looking to the Christ who now lives within—by yielding ourselves (spirit, soul, and body) to Him. A sanctified (holy) life is not achieved by our attempt to reform and improve the flesh (the old man). We have, by faith in Christ, put off the old man and have put on the new man. We are not indebted to the flesh (obligated to fulfill its desires). We were released from its bondage through the death of Jesus Christ who died for us. We are indebted to Jesus because He paid for our redemption. We owe Him our all, and therefore, we must give Him our undivided attention. If we set our minds on the flesh (even in an attempt to reform it), we will die. If we set our minds on the Spirit, we will live (Rom. 8:5–13).

Paul's epistle to the Colossians is written to correct the error of those who practice religious ceremonies and self-imposed restrictions on the flesh as a means of obtaining holiness. Of those practices Paul writes:

"Which things indeed have an appearance of wisdom in self-imposed religion, false humility, and neglect of the body, but are of no value against the indulgence of the flesh" (Col. 2:23).

In this epistle, Paul describes perfectly the way of the Christian life. Rather than quote the entire epistle, a few verses will be quoted here in hope these will entice the reader to study the epistle in its entirety.

> *For this reason we also, since the day we heard it, do not cease to pray for you, and to ask that you may be filled with the knowledge of His will in all wisdom and spiritual understanding; that you may walk worthy of the Lord, fully pleasing Him, being fruitful in every good work and increasing in the knowledge of God; strengthened with all might, according to His glorious power, for all patience and longsuffering with joy; giving thanks to the Father who has qualified us to be partakers of the saints in light.*
>
> *He has delivered us from the power of darkness and conveyed us into the kingdom of the Son of His love, in whom we have redemption through His blood, the forgiveness of sin.*
>
> *He is the image of the invisible God, the firstborn over all creation. For by Him all things were created that are in heaven and that are on Earth, visible and invisible, whether thrones or dominions or principalities or powers. All things were created through Him and for Him. And He is before all things, and in Him all things consist. And He is the head of the body, the church, who is the beginning, the firstborn from the dead, that in all things He may have the*

preeminence. For it pleased the Father that in Him all the fullness should dwell.

As you therefore have received Christ Jesus the Lord (by Faith), so walk in Him, rooted and built up in Him and established in the faith, as you have been taught, abounding in it with thanksgiving.

Let no one cheat you of your reward, taking delight in false humility and worship of angels, intruding into those things which he has not seen, vainly puffed up by his fleshly mind, and not holding fast to the Head, from whom all the body, nourished and knit together, grows with the increase that is from God.

If then you were raised with Christ, seek those things which are above, where Christ is, sitting at the right hand of God. Set you minds on things above, not on things on the Earth. For you died, and your life is hidden with Christ in God.

We, as believers, are God's new creations, and we are "complete in Him" (Col. 2:10). Let us, then, "lay aside every weight, and the sin which so easily ensnares us, and let us run with endurance the race that is set before us, looking unto Jesus the author and finisher of our faith, who for the joy that was set before Him endured the cross, despising the shame, and has sat down at the right hand of the throne of God" (Heb. 12:1–2). And we are more than conquerors through Him.

BELIEVERS ARE BORN OF GOD

The Spirit Himself bears witness with our spirit that we are children of God.

—R M. *8:16*

Believers are not only God's new creation in Christ Jesus and citizens of His kingdom, but they also have the awesome distinction of being the children of God, born of His Spirit.

"But as many as received Him, to them He gave the right to become children of God, to those who believe in His name: who were born, not of blood, nor of the will of the flesh, but of God" (John 3:12–13).

The nature of any living specie that distinguishes it from other living species is determined by its birth. Jesus said, "That which is born of the flesh is flesh, and that which is born of the Spirit is spirit" (John 3:6). This was in answer to Nicodemus's question, "How can a man be born when he is old [already born]?" Jesus explained that being born again was a new birth of the spirit, not the flesh. The new birth is a birth from above in which the Spirit of God is joined to the spirit of man making us one spirit with Him. "But he who is joined to the Lord is one spirit with Him" (1 Cor. 6:17).

We do not stop being man when we become Christians, but we do become a new type of man. The outer man is not changed. Outwardly, we are the same creatures we were before, living in the same bodies of flesh. It is the inward man (the man of the spirit) that is born of God and is a new creation in Christ Jesus.

"Therefore, if anyone is in Christ, he is a new creation; old things [things of the old man] have passed away; behold, all things have become new" (2 Cor. 5:17).

Just as we became part of the human family of the first man (Adam) by being birthed into it, we become part of the family of God by being born of God through the second Man (Jesus Christ). The first birth was of the flesh; the second birth is of the spirit. Our natural birth was through the seed of Adam; our spiritual birth is through the Seed of God.

Peter wrote, "Having been born again, not of corruptible seed but of incorruptible, through the Word of God which lives and abides forever" (1 Pet. 1:21).

"But we have this treasure in earthen vessels, that the excellence of the power may be of God and not of us" (2 Cor. 4:7).

"And so it is written, 'The first man Adam became a living being.' The last Adam became a life-giving spirit. However, the spiritual is not first, but the natural, and afterward the spiritual.

"The first man was of the Earth, made of dust; the second Man is the Lord from heaven. As was the man of dust, so also are those who are made of dust; and as is the heavenly man, so also are those who are heavenly. And as we have borne the image of the man of dust, we shall also bear the image of the heavenly Man" (1 Cor. 15:45–49).

It is important that we understand that we were not simply accepted by God and are, therefore, His people; we are born of God and are His children.

"The Spirit Himself bears witness with our spirit that we are children of God, and if children, then heirs—heirs of God and joint heirs with Christ, if indeed we suffer with Him, that we may also be glorified together" (Rom. 8:16–17).

Children of God are the heirs of God, not only eventually but also at the present time. Being heirs of God means we have an inheritance from Him. The Apostle Paul speaks of this in his epistle to the Ephesians.

"In Him [Christ], we have obtained [present tense] an inheritance, being predestined according to the purpose of Him who works all things according to the counsel of His will." This present inheritance, he says, is that of being sealed with the Holy Spirit of promise who is our guarantee of our future inheritance "until the redemption of the purchased possession." We are told in the book of Romans that the "redemption of the purchased possession" is "the adoption, the redemption of our body" which is the resurrection of our human bodies at the second coming of Christ.

Our present inheritance is the access we have currently to the things of God through the indwelling Spirit of Christ. This is what Jesus was referring to in His discourse with His disciples just before His crucifixion. He reminded them that He was going away and that there would be a period of darkness in which they would be filled with sorrow. He promised them that they would not be left alone for long because He was going to the Father, and when He had finished His work and was seated at the right hand of the Father, the Holy Spirit—One just like Himself—would come to be with as well as within them.

This would be greatly to their advantage. While Jesus was here bodily, He was limited in that He could not be everywhere with everyone at the same time. Also, there was not enough time for Him to teach them everything they needed to know. And because His work was not finished, there were things which could not be shared yet. Some of these things were beyond their natural ability to understand.

Jesus said, "I still have many things to say to you, but you cannot bear them now. However, when He, the Spirit of truth, has come, He will guide you into all truth; for He will not speak on His own authority, but whatever He hears He will speak; and He will tell you things to come. He will glorify Me, for He will take of what is Mine and declare it to you. All things that the Father has are mine. Therefore, I said that He will take of mine and declare it to you" (John 16:12–15).

We should also distinguish between being heirs and being joint heirs. Being individual heirs would indicate the inheritance is given to us as individuals and that we may use our own discretion as to what we do with them. Being joint heirs with Christ means we receive the things of God as joint owners with Christ. We have access to the things of God only as we are in Christ and in agreement with Him.

Jesus is "the firstborn among many brethren" (Rom. 8:29). Normally speaking, the firstborn would receive a double portion while the brethren would receive a portion. In this case, however, the entire inheritance is given to the firstborn, and the brethren have access to all they need in order to be successful in their assignment as related to the whole. Our inheritance in the things of God is not divided to us for us to own, but anything we need is available to us in the name of Jesus. How wonderful this is; we own nothing, yet we have access to everything!

This is also included in Jesus's discourse with His disciples. Speaking of the day when the Holy Spirit would be with them and would also be within them, Jesus said, "In that day you will ask Me nothing [will not ask questions of Me]. Most assuredly, I say to you, whatever you ask the Father in My name, He will give it you." To ask in His name is to ask what He would ask if He was doing the asking.

We are more than conquerors through Him who loved us because we are the children of God and, therefore, have access to all that He has.

WE ARE SAVED IN THIS HOPE

Not only that, but we also who have the firstfruits of the Spirit, even we ourselves groan within ourselves eagerly waiting for the adoption, the redemption of our body. For we were saved in this hope, but hope that is seen is not hope; for why does one still hope for what he sees? But if we hope for what we do not see, we eagerly wait for it with perseverance.

—ROM. 8:23–25

Here, we have another New Covenant reality that makes us more than conquerors. However, there are two words used here which must be defined according to the way they are used in the Bible and not as they are commonly used today. Otherwise, we will not understand what is taught here.

The word "hope" as it is commonly used means we anticipate something is going to happen, but there is a possibility it may not. "Hope" is used in the Scriptures to indicate that the thing promised is sure to happen when it is promised in the Word of God. We may confidently and patiently wait for it because it is based upon the Word of God who cannot lie. It will happen in His time. Furthermore, the waiting time is designed by the Lord to develop some needed character trait within the believer to prepare him for His eternal purpose.

The second word which needs to be interpreted according to its use in Scripture is "adoption." This word as used in Ephesians 1:5, Galatians 4:5, and Romans 8:23 means "to place as sons." In these verses, adoption is anticipated, not already fulfilled. In Ephesians 1:5, believers are said to be "predestined" to adoption as sons. In Romans 8:23, adoption is to take place at the redemption of our bodies (resurrection).

Adoption, then, is an anticipated event (hope) which will take place at the second coming of Christ when the dead in Christ will be resurrected, and those saints who are alive at that time will be changed. Both will be gloriously changed: "For our citizenship is in heaven, from which we also eagerly wait for the Savior, the Lord Jesus Christ, who will transform our lowly body that it may be conformed to His glorious body, according to the working by which He is able even to subdue all things to Himself" (Phil. 3:20–21).

"God does not adopt believers as children. They are begotten as such by His Holy Spirit through faith. Adoption is a term involving the dignity of the relationship of believers as sons. It is not a putting into the family by spiritual birth, but a putting into the position of sons" (W. E. Vine, Expository Dictionary of New Testament Words Zondervan).

The adoption (placing as sons) is positioning the sons of God who are matured, trained, and equipped to reign with Christ over the works of God's hands. They were manifested as His sons by the shining of the glory of the Father when they returned with Christ after the rapture. They are honored as coregents with Christ.

This hope in which we are saved is made sure in that it is the work of the triune God (God the Father, God the Son, and God the Holy Spirit). God the Father chose us in Christ before the foundation of the world and predestined us to be conformed to the image of Christ, making it a settled matter in eternity. He, Himself, determined that we should be holy and without blemish before Him in love.

God the Son, having finished the work of our redemption, gave us His Spirit of resurrection life and entered the Holy of Holies in the presence of the Father where He ever lives to make intercession for us.

God the Holy Spirit, having baptized us into the body of Christ, now indwells us as the Spirit of adoption, drawing us upward by revealing to us the things of Christ, transforming us into His likeness. This revelation involves showing us what we are in Christ and what He is in us. He helps us to see what we are now in the spirit and draws us upward toward what we shall be. In our finite understanding, we can only see dimly what we are destined to be, but the more revelation we receive, the more we are transformed. When Christ appears, and our eyes are opened to see Him as He is, we shall be like Him.

The Holy Spirit is the "earnest," the "firstfruit," the "foretaste" of the glory that shall be revealed in us. As the "Spirit of adoption," He draws us toward our destiny of being completely conformed to the likeness of Christ. What He is within us now will completely consume our total being, spirit, soul, and body.

This upward pull is what completely captivated and compelled the Apostle Paul. He tells us about it in his letter to the Philippians:

But what things were gain to me, these I have counted loss for Christ. Yet indeed I also count all things loss for the excellence of the knowledge of Christ Jesus my Lord, for whom I have suffered the loss of all things, and do count them as rubbish, that I may gain Christ and be found in Him, not having my own righteousness, which is by the law, but that which is through faith in Christ, the righteousness which is from God by faith; that I may know Him and the power of His resurrection, and the fellowship of His sufferings, being conformed to His death, if by any means, I may attain to the resurrection from the dead. Not that I have already attained, or am already perfected; but I press on, that I may lay hold of that for which Christ Jesus has laid hold of me.

Brethren, I do not count myself to have apprehended; but one thing I do, forgetting those things which are behind and reaching forward to those things which are ahead, I press toward the goal for the prize of the upward call of God in Christ Jesus.

—Phil. 3:7–14

This same upward call is in every believer. The Spirit of adoption constantly reveals more and more of Christ to us. The more we see of Him, the more we are attracted to Him. The Holy Spirit uses different means to reveal Christ to us. He uses Scripture; the gifts of apostles, prophets, evangelists, pastors, and teachers; the expressions of Christ through the lives of other Christians; and many other means. He also uses conditions, circumstances, and situations to teach and train us. All this to prepare us for the hope set before us.

This "hope" in which we are saved is twofold: number one is our transformation into the image of Christ which will be completed when He appears.

"Behold what manner of love the Father has bestowed upon us, that we should be called children of God! Therefore, the world does not know us, because it did not know Him. Beloved, now we are children of God; and it has not yet been revealed what we shall be, but we know that when He is revealed, we shall be like Him, for we shall see Him as He is. And everyone who has this hope purifies himself, just as He is pure" (1 John 3:1–3).

Number two, these brethren, who are conformed to His image, with Christ as the firstborn will be crowned with glory and honor to reign with Him over the works of God's hands.

If we endure, we shall reign with Him. (2 Tim. 2:12)

For He has not put the world to come, of which we speak, in subjection to angels. But one testified in a certain place, saying: What is man that You are mindful of him, or the son of man that You take care of him? You made him a little lower than the angels; You have crowned him with glory and honor, and set him over the works of your hands. You have put all things under his feet. For in that He put all in subjection under him, He left nothing that is not put under him. But now we do not yet see all things put under him.

But we see Jesus, who was made a little lower than the angels, for the suffering of death crowned with glory and honor, that He, by the grace of God, might taste death for everyone. For it was fitting for Him, for whom are

> *all things and by whom are all things, in bringing many*
> *sons to glory, to make the captain of their salvation perfect*
> *through sufferings. For both He who sanctifies and those*
> *who are sanctified are all of one, for which reason He is*
> *not ashamed to call them brethren.*
>
> —*HEB. 2:5–11*

Jesus has already received all authority in heaven and on Earth. Someday, He will return to Earth with the manifested sons of God to reign over the works of God's hands. That is the fulfillment of the hope in which we are saved, the anticipated adoption, the placing as sons of the manifested sons of God.

The first aspect of this hope is equally true of every believer. Every believer will be perfectly holy—without spot, wrinkle, or any such thing. Everyone who is taken up to meet Jesus in the air will be perfected in holiness. All that is not of Him will fall away as we see Him as He is. Everyone will be like Him, but no one will be equal to Him. All will be like Him in kind, but some will be greater in status than others.

The difference in status is because some have been more submissive and obedient than others. God needs obedient sons to whom He can entrust the administering of the works of His hands. Obedient sons do what their Father tells them to do.

We will be rewarded according to how much we have allowed the Holy Spirit to accomplish within us and through us. Those who diligently pursue the Lord—those who seek to know Him intimately—will be worthy of more reward because they gave up more for Him. They gave Him more glory; consequently, they will receive more glory. Their reward will be greater glory to be of greater service in His kingdom.

Paul spoke of this difference in glory when speaking of the resurrection:

> *There are also celestial bodies and terrestrial bodies; but the glory of the celestial is one, and the glory of the terrestrial is another. There is one glory of the sun, another glory of the moon, and another glory of the stars; for one star differs from another star in glory.*
>
> *So also is the resurrection of the dead. The body is sown in corruption, it is raised in incorruption. It is sown in dishonor, it is raised in glory. It is sown in weakness, it is raised in power. It is sown a natural body, it is raised a spiritual body. There is a natural body, and there is a spiritual body.*
>
> —*1 Cor. 15:40–44*

Our resurrected bodies are compared to heavenly bodies. All the heavenly bodies shine with brilliance, but some are more brilliant than others. They all rule; some rule the day while others rule the night according to their purpose.

All believers are called "holy brethren, partakers of the heavenly calling." Some respond more completely and more readily than others. God is no respecter of persons. He desires the best and highest for all His children. But He can only reward us according to our works. Rewards are given, not according to our accomplishments but according to how faithful we have been with what He called us to do.

That is why the Apostle Paul was careful that he labors only where the Lord had appointed him. He wrote to the church at Corinth, "We, however, will not boast beyond measure, but within the limits of the sphere which God appointed us—a sphere which includes especially you. For we are not overextending ourselves [as though our authority did not extend to you] for it was to you that we came with the gospel of Christ" (2 Cor. 10:13–14). Obedience is more important than earthly recognition.

The apostle also wrote:

> *I planted, Apollos watered, but God gave the increase. Now he who plants and he who waters are one, and each one will receive his own reward according to his own labor. For we are God's fellow workers; you are God's building. According to the grace of God which was given to me, as a wise master builder I have laid the foundation, and another builds on it. But let each one take heed how he builds on it. For no other foundation can anyone lay than that which is laid, which is Jesus Christ.*
>
> *Now if anyone builds on this foundation with gold, silver, precious stones, wood, hay, straw, each one's work will become clear, for the day will declare it, because it will be revealed by fire; and the fire will test each one's work of what sort it is. If anyone's work which he has built on it endures, he will receive a reward. If anyone's work is burned, he will suffer loss; but he himself will be saved, yet so as by fire.*
>
> *—1 Cor. 3:6–15*

God the Father, God the Son, and God the Holy Spirit (the triune God) is involved in bringing this hope in which we are saved to completion. Since God cannot fail, we are more than conquerors through Him who loves us.

GROANINGS

*For we know that the whole creation groans and labors
with birth pangs until now. Not only that, but we also who
have the firstfruits of the Spirit, even we ourselves, eagerly
waiting for the adoption, the redemption of our body.*

—ROM. 8:22–23

There are three "groanings" referred to in Romans
chapter 8; the two mentioned in the verses quoted above
and the one in verse 26. First, we have the groaning of
creation; that is, the groans which can be seen and heard
in nature. The things around us, the animal kingdom, the
elements (the air, earth, etc.), as well as the plant kingdom
are not as they were when God created them and saw that
what He had created was "good."

We see and hear the groaning of creation in the howling
of the wind as tornadoes and other types of storms ravage
the Earth; in the shaking of the earth as plates shift and
rocks are rent; in lack of production in deserts and barren
wilderness; in the overgrowth of the jungle; in worthless
weeds and brambles which choke out useful plants; in
the terror of animals as ravenous wolves and others tear
and destroy; and thousands of other destructive forces
that war against one another. We see it among men who
bite and devour each other, sickness, suffering, and death
which is the common lot of man and beast. All these (and
millions more) are the groanings of nature as the result of

the curse which came upon the creation of God as a result of sin which entered the world through man.

No one who believes in the God of the Bible could believe things are as He created them nor that He will allow things to continue as they are. Eventually, in God's own time and according to His eternal purpose, the Son of God will be revealed from heaven with a host of manifested sons of God who will reign with Him as He delivers creation from the bondage of corruption into the glorious liberty of the sons of God. The wolf and the lamb shall feed together, the desert shall blossom as the rose, men will "beat their swords into plowshares, and their spears into pruning hooks; nation shall not lift up sword against nation, neither shall they learn war anymore" (Isa. 2:4). The kingdoms of this world will become the kingdom of our God and of His Anointed (Christ, Messiah), as He rules them with a rod of iron. His kingdom of peace and righteousness shall cover the whole Earth as His royal law of love becomes the way of life.

All of creation groans as it awaits this unveiling of the sons of God. We who have received the firstfruits of the Spirit of adoption also groan within ourselves as we eagerly wait for the completion of the adoption—the redemption of our bodies. This is the hope into which we were saved.

> *For I consider that the sufferings of this present time are not worthy to be compared with the glory which shall be revealed in us. For the earnest expectation of the creation eagerly waits for the revealing of the sons of God. For the creation was subjected to futility, not willingly, but because of Him who subjected it in hope; because the creation itself also will be delivered from the bondage of corruption into*

the glorious liberty of the children of God. For we know that the whole creation groans and labors with birth pangs together until now.

Not only that, but we also who have received the firstfruits of the Spirit, even we ourselves groan within ourselves, eagerly waiting for the adoption, the redemption of our body.

—Rom. 8:18–23

And then, we have the other groaning—that of the Holy Spirit. God has not left us to face the storms of life alone. Nothing can come our way that our Father is not aware of nor that He is not, Himself, intimately involved in with us.

Jesus promised His followers that He would not leave us orphaned but that He would pray the Father and He would send another Comforter, another just like Himself, who would be with us and in us forever.

True to His promise, He sent the Holy Spirit to be with us and within us always and everywhere. He is in our hearts to guide and strengthen us, and He surrounds us to protect and keep us. He leads us where we need to go and brings things our way which will develop and fashion us. He provides brothers and sisters to edify and encourage us; He allows our enemies to provoke and try us. He leads us beside still waters to refresh and restore us; He leads us through troubled waters to teach us obedience and endurance.

We do not always know what is needed to bring us to full maturity in Christ, but the Holy Spirit does. Not knowing what is needed, we do not know how to pray. Should we pray to be delivered from the situation we are in, or should we pray to be strengthened as we endure it?

At this point, the Holy Spirit is our Helper. He takes hold together with us, and by identifying with our groaning, He intercedes for us, praying with groanings which cannot be uttered (put into intelligible words). God the Father, who searches the motives of the heart and knows the mind of the Spirit (that He is praying through us what is according to the will of God), answers our prayer.

By means of this intercessory ministry, God is able to orchestrate events and situations in our experience which always works out for our good. This must not be misconstrued to teach that all things work out for good for everyone. This fallacy, which is responsible for the destruction of countless millions who have rested in its false security, can be exposed by simply asking Judas Iscariot if everything worked out for his good!

The Bible does not say, "Everything works for good." What the Bible teaches is that "all things work together for good to those who love God, to those who are the called according to His purpose" (Rom. 8:28). Those who love God and are called according to His purpose are those who have repented of their sins, have received Jesus Christ as Savior and Lord, and in whose hearts dwells the Spirit of Christ as the Spirit of adoption, drawing them upward conforming them to His image. The "all things" of their life experiences work together for their good because the Holy Spirit coordinates them as instruments to help mold and fashion them through faith and patience.

These "things" work more efficiently when we learn to pray in the spirit for one another and for ourselves. Praying is not intended as a way for us to get our fleshly lusts fulfilled, but the way to get God's will done on

Earth as it is in heaven. This type of praying is not an insincere utterance of words of indifference but is an actual, heartfelt involvement with God as His partners to accomplish His will.

To utter the words "thy will be done" without a sincere, heartfelt desire to see God's will done is to make mockery of prayer. Those words, uttered by Jesus in the Garden of Gethsemane, was His "nevertheless." His desire was that the Father's will be done, no matter how much pain it cost Him. He was in such agony He sweat drops of blood; His pain was so great He was at the point of death; nevertheless, because through this pain the world would be reconciled to God, and because this would bring good to all who would believe in Him, and because the whole economy of God (God's eternal purpose) depended upon Him drinking this cup, He prayed, "Not My will, but Thine be done."

In like manner (but on a much smaller scale), when we come upon situations which are painful (and costly) to our flesh, we must "pray it through" until we can sincerely say, "Not my will, but Thine be done." This will always turn out to our good.

Here is a biblical example which shows us how this works. There was a man in Christ who was caught up to the third heaven where he received much revelation of things known only to God until that time. When this man began to share these things with others, the natural tendency would be for men to exalt him above the measure God had for him; and even within himself, there would be the temptation to think of himself more highly than he should, bringing harm to himself.

God, because He loved the man and wanted to prevent him from harm, allowed him to be given "a thorn in the flesh, the messenger of Satan," to buffet him, to keep him humble.

We are not told exactly what this "thorn" was; however, we can know something of what it was like. We know it was unpleasant because it buffeted him. We know, according to 2 Corinthians 12:10, it was stressful; it involved persecution; it involved insufficiency; it brought reproaches; and it involved infirmities.

The man, knowing the Lord could remove the thorn, prayed for it to be removed. When the thorn was not removed (as he had expected), the man prayed a second time for the thorn to be removed. The thorn was still not removed; the situation was still the same. Knowing that the living God hears and answers prayer, and being in earnest about this matter, the man prayed a third time. This time, he received an answer but not the answer he had expected. (Which reveals the fact that he did not know how to pray as he ought about this matter.)

The answer came in the form of a message from the Lord, "My grace is sufficient for you, for My strength is made perfect in weakness" (2 Cor. 12:9).

The Lord had something better for the man than what he was asking. Had the Lord given the man what he was asking, the situation would have changed, but the man himself would have remained the same. It is better for him to experience the power of God's sustaining grace in the face of his own limitations.

To illustrate: let us suppose the problem the man faced was that he was being persecuted. In such a situation, the man may not be able, in his own strength, to love those who are persecuting him, but God can! By allowing God's grace to function enabling him to love his enemies and do good to those who are persecuting him, the persecutor may be brought to repentance and become a follower of Christ. In that way, the persecuted has gained a friend, and Christ has gained a follower. If the persecutor does not repent but continues to persecute, the one being persecuted for righteousness will receive his reward from the Lord—he cannot lose. He is more than conqueror through Him who loves him! And in addition to that, in receiving the gift of God's sustaining grace the believer becomes "partaker of the divine nature."

> *Grace and peace be multiplied to you in the knowledge of God and of Jesus our Lord, as His divine power has given to us all things that pertain to life and godliness, through the knowledge of Him who called us by glory and virtue, by which have been given to us exceedingly great and precious promises, that through these you may be partakers of the divine nature, having escaped the corruption that is in the world through lust.*
>
> —2 PET. 1:3–4

Paul—the man in Christ to whom was given the thorn in the flesh—upon hearing that the Lord's strength is made perfect in our weakness, responded, "Therefore most gladly I will rather boast in my infirmities, that the power of Christ may rest upon me. Therefore, I take pleasure in infirmities, in needs, in persecutions, in distresses, for Christ's sake. For when I am weak, then I am strong" (2

Cor. 12:9–10). And that makes us more than conquerors through Him who loves us!

CLOSING ARGUMENTS

One of the best ways to settle a matter and bring it to finality is, after having presented irrefutable evidence, ask questions to which the answer is obvious based on the evidence. That is exactly what is done in the eighth chapter of the book of Romans.

We might refer to these as review questions for the final exam. The good thing about review questions is that they help us discover areas where improvement is needed. If we don't know the answer to the question, we can go to the text and find the correct answer. This is not the case with the final exam. The final exam is final!

The series of questions asked in Romans 8:31–35, to which the answers are obvious based on the evidence presented in the previous verses, is more than adequate to settle the matter of security for believers. The first question, "What shall we then say to these things?" is designed to cause us to reflect on the evidence which has been presented. The next question, "If God be for us, who can be against us?" is the overarching question which leaves us in absolute awe! Who could successfully compete against God? And God is on our side? Or is He? He is if we are on His side. God will always be for us unless we oppose Him. Those who oppose God are surely on the losing side. But we have chosen to be His through Jesus Christ; therefore, God is for us!

"He who did not spare His own Son, but delivered Him up for us all, how shall He not with Him also freely give us all things?" is the next mind-expanding question. Why would God give us the most precious thing He had and then deny us anything of less value? We can rest assured that whatever we need, we can freely receive from Him who loves us so.

The next awesome questions have to do with accusations. There is an "accuser of the brethren" who does all he can to keep us from enjoying the freedom we have in the presence of our Father. He and his helpers constantly seek to remind us of our unworthiness by bringing accusations against us, some of which are true and some false. There are two reasons why we are more than conquerors when these accusations are made.

In the first place, the chief justice on the super supreme court, before whom the accusations are made, is the one who himself "justifies the ungodly" (Rom. 4:5). In the second place, the means by which He justifies the ungodly is by giving His own Son, Jesus Christ the righteous, as a sacrifice to die for the ungodly (Rom. 5:6), and furthermore, His Son has been resurrected from the dead and is in the courtroom to intercede for the accused as their Advocate. This Advocate (our defense attorney) is there, not to plead our innocence but to plead His blood for our forgiveness through the propitiation that is in His blood. He Himself bore our sins on the cross and now offers His blood as proof of our redemption and that we are reconciled to God by His blood.

"Who is he who condemns?" (There is no condemnation) For "it is Christ who died, and furthermore, is also risen, who is at the right hand of God, who also makes intercession for us" (Rom. 8:34). Hey, this thing is rigged in our favor! Case closed; end of issue.

Concluding question (in light of these New Covenant realities),

> *"Who shall separate us from the love of Christ? Shall tribulation, or distress, or persecution, or famine, or nakedness, or peril, or sword? As it is written: "For your sake we are killed all day long; we are accounted as sheep for the slaughter."*
>
> *Nay, in all these things we are more than conquerors through Him who loved us, for I am persuaded that neither death nor life, nor angels nor principalities nor powers, nor things present nor things to come, nor height nor depth, nor any other created thing, shall be able to separate us from the love of God which is in Christ Jesus our Lord.*
>
> *—Rom. 8:35–39*

> *Therefore, my beloved brethren, be steadfast, immovable, always abounding in the work of the Lord, knowing that your labor is not in vain in the Lord.*
>
> *—1 Cor. 15:58)*